# THE NARROW DOORWAY

my extraordinary life

**SANDY PHILLIPS**

Sandy Phillips © 2014

All rights reserved

No parts of this publication may be reproduced, stored in a retrieval system, or transmitted in any form or by any means whatsoever without the prior permission of the publisher.
A record of this publication is available from the British Library.

ISBN 978-1-907203-98-5

Typesetting by Wordzworth Ltd
*www.wordzworth.com*

Cover design by Titanium Design Ltd
*www.titaniumdesign.co.uk*

Printed by Lightning Source UK
*www.lightningsource.com*

Cover image: The Spider Web Nebula © Sandra Phillips

Published by Local Legend
*www.local-legend.co.uk*

This book is dedicated to my
understanding and supportive husband,
to my mother and to my family.

# About This Book

This is the story of a life that began at the start of World War II.

The spiritual things that happened to Sandy, the animals and people from other times that she saw, were as far as she was aware happening to everyone. It was all part of living an ordinary life. She knew nothing of her grandmother's and mother's psychic abilities or interests but in her early twenties got to know more about her grandmother and was able to call on her when she needed help and strength to manage the pain in her life. She accompanied her mother to spiritual meetings but was not really aware of what it was all about.

This all changed as she grew older with increasing psychic experiences and indeed the intrusion into her life of some dark entities, causing her much fear. For a long time she blocked her natural mediumship, until religious faith strengthened her. Here, for the first time, Sandy tells the story of an utterly extraordinary life in which this world may have changed beyond recognition but the spirit world speaks to us with an unerring message: we are not alone and we never die!

# The Author

Sandy always wanted to be an artist, an actor, dancer or poet. She has written and painted for as long as she can remember, and along the way has also been an actor and teacher. Seeing the spirit world has gone hand in hand with everything she has done.

She had three major ambitions in life. One was to have a piece of art work exhibited at the Royal Academy and the second was to write a book. With *The Narrow Doorway* she has now achieved these two. The third ambition is to be closer to a spiritual life.

# Acknowledgements

To Nigel Peace for his patience and
help in writing this book.

*www.local-legend.co.uk*

# Beginning

BANG! The house shook and parts of the ceiling fell onto my bed where I was fast asleep. Windows imploded and sent splinters of glass spraying around the now dark room. I cried because I didn't know what was happening. My mother stuffed my arms into a warm coat, saying that it was alright but we had to go. She picked me up and ran into the night. As she went past the public house across the road to our flat, she saw her friend lying decapitated and with all her limbs detached. She pressed my head into her shoulder so that this terrible vision was blocked. I clearly remember this though at the time of course I did not know why. As she ran with me, the noise of a Doodle Bug hummed above us and then stopped. These bombs were supposed to fall once the engine had stopped. My mother tried to find cover under the arch of a large door. An angel must have been looking down on us right then because it started up again and moved off, only to fall some distance away from us.

We were both saved that night in more ways than one. My mother told me years later that she used to pop over to the pub each night to get some cigarettes and have a quick word with her friend who served behind the bar. However, this particular night, she told me, a voice kept saying in her ear not to go, "There's a lot of ironing to be done." This was repeated a few times and so she didn't go. It was while she was ironing that the bomb fell onto the pub. We both owe our lives to spirit.

I was six years old when I saw my first ghost. It wasn't anything spectacular like a transparent vision with a ghastly wail or drooling face; indeed I wasn't even aware that it was a ghost at all. The fact that it wasn't even human didn't bother me because horses in those days were quite run of the mill. It just stood there in a brilliant white aura, swishing its long tail.

I was coming home from Sunday School accompanied by my cousin who never stopped talking and I had just sort of cut off. We walked into Alwyne Square where my mother and I lived with an old aunt, having just returned to London from Devizes where we had been evacuated. The Square had only one way in and out and in the centre was an oval shaped green area with overgrown grass and beautiful mature trees. The horse stood by some ruins with its back to us. As we entered, it turned and looked at us as if wondering who was making all the noise. I remarked on the beauty of the horse before me, cutting in on my cousin's babble. Marie looked and saw nothing so she asked me where it was, and turned to look behind her. "There, just by the ruins," I told her, turning to point to where it was standing. However, to my amazement, it had disappeared. She couldn't see any horse and denied that there was anything. It couldn't have escaped because of the layout of the area, for there were bombed houses on one side and the remaining houses on the other.

We ran home to tell my mother, who listened very carefully. She said to come and show her exactly where I saw it. We all walked outside with Marie constantly repeating that she didn't see a horse. I showed my mother the location and all she said was that it was strange.

She did, however, believe me and it wasn't until years later that she told me what had occurred previously. The day before I saw the horse, my mother had met an old gentleman over by the bombed ruins. They had been chatting about the old days generally and he told her that he had once lived in the house that was now a bombed ruin, opposite to where we lived, and that he had once possessed a beautiful white horse and trap to convey him around town. My mother had not talked to me about this chance meeting, in fact she had never mentioned the spirit world at all to me. After this first sighting, she did.

# Life

*She hovered, hesitating above the woman.*
*Must she do this?*
*She had been quite content watching eternity go by.*
*Something drew her closer,*
*she was aware of the woman's pain.*
*No, she didn't want to do this.*
*Life for her had been a terrible effort.*
*A voice came softly to her,*
*"It will be different this time,*
*other trials to bear, oh yes, but different."*
*The woman below her moaned.*
*She held her large taut stomach tightly.*
*A voice said, "Big effort now, push!"*
*Time ticked by,*
*she wasn't sure about this at all.*
*She tried to leave, but an invisible thread*
*held her close to the woman,*
*pulling her nearer each minute.*
*Suddenly the thread fell loose.*
*The woman went silent.*
*She felt panic play across the room.*
*"We're going into theatre," shouted someone,*
*"Get the anaesthetist."*

*They quickly pushed the woman on a trolley*
*into a silver white room.*
*She soared through the air,*
*hurrying to keep up with her.*
*'Poor woman, nothing is easy in life,' she thought.*
*She watched as they made an incision.*
*Blood ran, machines purred.*
*"How's she doing?" a man inquired.*
*Another nodded, "Fine".*
*She felt the thread pull again, stronger this time.*
*She was slipping, sliding away,*
*falling faster, and towards the pink and red.*
*There was a whoosh sound; she started to cry,*
*a thin hollow cry that filled the room.*
*She was born again.*

My mother told me one thing very early on about believing in spirit: "Thoughts are things." That is, if you think bad thoughts it is as good as doing it. She gave me an example. At her place of work there was a woman with whom she could not get on. Mum actually thought of something bad to happen to her and a few days after this the woman's little daughter came out in strange spots and was ill, baffling her doctors. My mother was immediately really sorry she had thought bad things about her. She didn't want to harm a child. She asked for forgiveness of spirit and just as quickly the woman's child got better. So I have always tried not to think bad things. I fail many times, of course, but I always try.

As a young child I always saw auras around people and animals. I never asked about it, I presumed everyone saw what I saw. It's only when you lose the ability do you realise what a wonderful gift you had. After many years I began to see them again only very faintly, nothing like the beautiful colours I used to see. I continued seeing animals in spirit form at first: cats, birds and dogs and the like. However, one day

# BEGINNING

coming home from school I saw a lion! He was sitting in someone's front garden seeming to gaze out over the veldt. I was most excited and ran to tell Mum as usual. Once I even saw a rhinoceros, which was to be confirmed much later in my life; I met a gentleman whose company was drilling a bore hole deep down in Trafalgar Square and he told me that tiny bone fragments of rhino and other animals had been found.

When coming home from the pictures one night, I looked into a narrow doorway and saw the bottom half of a man. The doorway was too narrow to contain a real man and so I was quite frightened by this. I was lagging behind Mum as usual, and I ran to catch up with her to tell her. She replied that it was only a spirit beginning to form and just hadn't completed it yet. I must say that this was the first time I had been frightened by what I saw. I was really very lucky to have my mother as a mother. She never mocked me or disbelieved what I told her. She and my maternal grandmother were Spiritualists.

It was as I grew a little older that my mother took me to spiritual meetings. The one I really remember was held near Holborn and I remember that the medium was Ronald Strong.

Two of my own children are mediums today, although I was cautious about the movement when they were young. My son Jeff is known as 'The psychic postman' on Facebook and is at his happiest serving in spiritual churches. He travels quite a long way to do medium platform work. He is a very happy and cheerful worker and really knows how to lift the atmosphere. My daughter Julie does more one-to-one readings and has only just started to go on the platform. Both are very gifted. The three of us have done work for charity, once raising some money for a girl to go to Africa to help in an orphanage and other times we have raised money for the Noah's Ark Hospice for Children. My other son Simon used to think that it was all rubbish, but nowadays he seems more than a little interested. He does however support the other two when they try to do something special. His talents lay in another direction of a more academic and practical path.

# THE NARROW DOORWAY

When I was young, aunts, uncles and teachers always reported that I had a great imagination, and I did. I saw witches made from an old dressing gown that hung on a hook in my bedroom; the stars in the night sky were my fairies; shadows danced as creatures of all sorts on the wall; but really I knew that it was my imagination. I knew the spirit world was not.

We lived in a very old, large house in the lower ground part which had been the servants' quarters. I know this because we still had the bell system that rang to say who was needed by the upper class people above. It had one gas mantle in the kitchen that gave out a very low light. There was also an old black range on which my aunt always had a kettle hung over the fire. The rest of the house was in darkness when the sun went down so we went everywhere by candle. I did hate this. We had a tin bath by the fire every week, whether we needed it or not. We had to fill the copper boiler that was in the scullery and cart it by the bucket to the kitchen to empty into the bath. In other ways I loved this old house. It had a grand staircase outside leading to the upper story, with a square pattern tiled pathway up to it on which I could keep my whip and top spinning for a long time.

In my aunt's bedroom, one of the first floor rooms, there was a wonderful mirror. To me it was enormous, with a high mantelpiece. Golden columns rose up around it with oval discs picturing ladies in crinoline dresses dancing with men in silk knee britches, all coloured in pastel shades. Alas, it has been knocked down now. I had plenty of stimuli around me.

# My Ups and Downs with Spirit

Later in life I went with a couple I knew to meet a few of their friends intending to use the planchette, or ouija board. The usual glass with fingers on, spelling out odd messages, went on. One message given to one of the girls whom I didn't know was, 'Give Darren an answer.' An answer to what? The message spelled out, 'Marriage.' "I don't even like Darren," she laughed. Funnily enough she did end up marrying him a few years later.

But I do not advocate using the ouija nowadays. People tend to take it lightly, as a joke, and it certainly isn't that. My mother and I used it quite a bit but one day something came up that was definitely not nice and we never used it again. This occurrence opened a door to many situations later on in life. Some experiences crept in under the guise of being pleasant but turned extremely nasty and I was plagued by them for years. Eventually they were cleared away by my faith in God. I literally saw His hand come and flick away the tormenter as if it were a fly. My nights are much more peaceful now but I am reluctant to talk or write about these experiences now because I believe that the ouija board is dangerous. It opens a doorway to anything on 'the other side'. If you do not take the appropriate steps to protect yourself, anything can become attached to you. My mother had mental problems in later life and I do

## THE NARROW DOORWAY

wonder if it was because of that one time. Dear reader, I do beg you not to go down this avenue. It is because of all this that I became reluctant to delve too deeply into psychic matters; if I do readings for charity I feel safer, as I do with family and friends. Over the past few years, however, I have had a return of confidence.

I did move house quite a bit with my mother and in one run-down hotel I kept seeing the same face at night. It was the head of a man, just the head, but so very vivid in colour, more colour than in real life. He would be staring at me when I woke in the middle of the night but I never found out about him. He was just there, not happy, not sad nor angry, but he used to scare me. I would be lying on my back in the dark of night and I just opened my eyes to see a head with hypnotic blue eyes staring down at me from a few inches above my nose. I quickly pulled the covers over my head! Luckily I had no trouble going back to sleep. Another night I was lying on my side and the same thing happened, face a few inches from me. He definitely invaded my personal space.

My mother was due to marry a Polish man and they had found a downstairs flat in Kensington. I would travel there to visit from the hotel. However, I hated this flat and refused to stay there at night. When my mother told me where I was to sleep I was even more determined to leave. There was an enormous boiler in my bedroom with a cot (a very narrow bed) for me. It was extremely dark in there even with the lights on. To get from the kitchen to the front room you had to go through my bedroom which was closed off by a large dark red curtain. I felt as if bodies had been cut up and stuffed in the boiler, which was also in the far part of my room. This last part might have been my imagination at work but it still horrified me.

In the kitchen there was a constant smell of 'monkey' and a feeling of agitation. It definitely had a dark aura in there. In other rooms a feeling of evil struck me. In due course the engagement fell through and my mother only then told me about an old woman who had once lived there and kept a monkey in the place. Mum also talked about a voice that spoke to her as she was going to clean a room and wondering if she had everything. The voice asked her, "Have you got everything?" She confessed that she hadn't liked the place either as many other voices had whispered to her. They had been quite hostile but she didn't elaborate on them.

One evening my mother had invited a work mate to visit so that she could do some medium work for her. I was in the room just reading, not paying any attention, when suddenly I became freezing cold and started to cry. I looked up towards my mother who had spoken to me and I saw a sledge sliding down a hill. I told her and she just hustled me into the bathroom to get a hot bath. When I emerged the friend had gone and her story had been told to Mum. It happened that her father had made a sledge for a little boy who lived next door. The boy had used it and had slid onto an icy pond and it had sunk. The boy had died. Her father, now deceased, wanted to tell her that he was with him and they were both fine.

Each Christmas we had a small tree which was decorated with the usual balls and tinsel and was placed on a table in front of the window. Mum had the spirit of a young black child who was always with her, especially at Christmas, and this spirit loved playing with the items on the decorated tree. I would watch the tinsel move and the balls spin around. However I was reluctant to accept this and said it was the wind. I must have been at that perverse teenage stage, because I used to put my hand all around the window feeling for a draught. However, one night when we sat admiring the glitter and glow I did hear some laughing coming from that vicinity which sounded just like a young child and I had to admit defeat to my mother. Even today I still watch my Christmas tree, eager to see if one of my guides or my mother would move the baubles. I think I have seen it but then maybe I'm willing them to move.

This poem was started off for me by a spirit of a young cockney lad. I wasn't trying to contact anyone, he just stepped in. The impression that he gave to me was that this is how he thought until he passed over and found things very different.

# Dead As...

*Nah! Don't believe in that,*
*when yer's dead, yer's dead,*
*ain't no such fing as a spirit, ghost, whatever,*
*that rises up and goes to 'eaven.*
*Nah, when yer's dead, yer's dead.*
*Yer bones and fings just rot in the muck,*
*the worms come in and finish yer up,*
*yer just become earth and bits,*
*then trees an' flowers an' carrots*
*can grow in yer. Yer can live again*
*in that kind of way, sort of, but*
*when yer's dead, yer's dead.*
*Nah, there ain't no such fings as ghosts,*
*they're made up fings to frighten kids.*
*Don't scare me,*
*don't mind seeing 'em on the flicks though,*
*me an me bird went to see a zombie one once,*
*she got scared an' cuddled in, close like,*
*great, she sort of likes scary fings.*
*Me, nah, when yer's dead, yer's dead.*
*No God, no ghosts, zombies, spirits,*
*least that's what I fink. Don't you?*
*But when me Dad died, in the army like,*
*me Ma, she sort of knew. Said she saw 'im,*
*make's yer fink, don't it.*

# Time to Move On

This story is not strictly psychic but it's interesting. When I married and had my second child I was up on the flat-topped roof, hanging nappies between the chimney pots. This was in 1961 and I hadn't a garden or a drying machine then. I looked up into a clear blue sky, sun shining, and saw a large UFO. Not that I thought that at the time. It was cigar-shaped with rounded ends. It was a beautiful, a gleaming golden colour. I stood and watched it and so did my daughter who was just a toddler. It drifted slowly from the west and then stopped for some seconds. I remember thinking that I wished it would come over and above me so I could tell what it was. As though reading my thoughts, it sped off to the north away from me so quickly it was gone almost immediately. That was strange, I thought, but I see so many strange things, it's just another one, and that was that. I went on about my busy life. However I have never forgotten it or the beauty of the colour. As time went on and there was much more information about this type of phenomenon, I realised what I'd seen.

Our family were just about to return home after a holiday when the thought of checking the tyres came to my mind. At that time I did not drive and knew nothing about the workings of a car. I vaguely said to my husband, "Are the tyres alright?" His return look was puzzled and he did not really answer me. However my concern

# THE NARROW DOORWAY

grew while travelling home. Half-way home we suddenly spun and with luck my husband was able to get onto the hard shoulder. On inspection we had experienced a blow-out. Go with your hunches, dear reader, you may well be right. I might add that he pays more attention to my odd comments nowadays.

At one time I was getting a lot of books from the library about witchcraft, not a wise thing to become absorbed with - questionable subject matter, as I found out. I was in the habit of meeting up with a girlfriend every now and then in a local pub for a chat. We would meet outside the establishment at a set time and go in together. I stood one day waiting for her as she was very late. Alongside me was a tall dark man who also looked as if he were waiting for someone. As one does, we got to talking about the absence of friends and having decided that they were both not going to turn up, he invited me in to have a drink. I accepted. We sat and talked and funnily enough witchcraft became a subject. When I decided that I should go, he offered me a lift home and again, very foolishly, I accepted. He drove me towards home but veered off to an out-of-the-way road. It was just a dirt track area really.

He stopped outside the Free Worship Church that I used to attend. Suddenly I was frozen, I mean really and absolutely, I could not move any part of my body. My mind was frozen too; I tried to make sense of it all but couldn't. My brain became a bird flapping its wings, frantic in its effort to get out of a cage. I was this bird in a cage but I could do nothing. I was terrified. He said, or transmitted mentally to me - somehow I heard the thoughts – "No, you're no good ,your brain is too weak." I was suddenly released from this paralysed state and scrambled out of the car thankfully and ran home without a backward glance, very glad to have been considered too weak in the head. I do believe that somehow, he and whoever his associates were, knew about me and was considering me as 'a new recruit'.

This experience could be taken as one of fantasy (it wasn't) but when I spoke to my girlfriend the next day, she told me her story. On her way to meet me by bus she was struck by abdominal pains. They were so bad that she decided to get off and cross over and get a bus back home. Once off the bus her pain stopped, so she decided to carry on and boarded the next bus towards our meeting spot. Once again the pains returned and she got off again. The pain stopped. She repeated the same sequence again and again she had to get off. The fourth time she did get off and went home. She told me the pains were very severe. I find that very strange and no fantasy. I never sought out information on witchcraft again. 'There are more things in Heaven and Hell...'

I once went into a local fair and on impulse went to the gypsy tent that stood in the corner of the field. She told me various things that I cannot recall now; this was about thirty-odd years ago. However the one piece that I didn't forget was the fact that I had been a witch in a previous life. She added that I knew that anyway. At the time I did wonder about this aspect but couldn't actually remember it. I stared hard at her when she told me this, and seeing my look she hastily added, "You were a white witch of course," and I relaxed. I've never wanted to hurt anyone or crave for power, only that which I obtained for myself.

This next piece of my story was exciting. I have had one out-of-body experience and I wrote a poem about it which tells what happened.

# Out of Body

*Light as air, I lifted from my body,*
*way, way above the Earth.*
*Travelling slowly at first, I headed north towards*
*great glaciers, between the mountains' girth,*
*as they lay sparkling away.*

## THE NARROW DOORWAY

*My spirit yearned for cool clean crystal air of Arctic,*
*with giant icebergs all brittle blue,*
*half submerged in a tranquil, turquoise sea,*
*quiet, peaceful, drifting in and out of view,*
*onward I fly, white binds my eye.*

*Yes, that's where I want to be, really,*
*the world far beneath me slowly spins,*
*countries, oceans, all, I quickly pass over in awe,*
*no heat or cold, just pure joy that sings,*
*happy just being and seeing.*

*Suddenly I am aware, this is too far, too fast.*
*Doubt and fear strike, this speed of travel… Wow,*
*I feel the invisible cord tug, ready to pull me back,*
*"No, no," I cry, "I don't want to go, not now."*
*Try to keep hold, thud, wake cold.*

*Dull, heavy, disappointed, trapped within,*
*in opposition to the light, carefree soaring soul.*
*Is this what it will be like? How wonderful.*
*Confined to memory, this vision holds my goal,*
*when Earthly chores are past, Heaven at last.*

Oh how I wanted to continue my journey to the north. I tried with all my might not to return to my body but that cord was strong. It seemed to me like a thick piece of elastic. I look forward to be able to travel around when I'm no longer in this life. Although, I hasten to add, I'm not eager to advance to that state.

I always loved dancing and used to go to a lot of dinner dances with various people. My husband would jive with me but he couldn't really do ballroom style dancing. He did an odd waltz to everything else. I found that I could do a quickstep with one friend, a Charleston with another and my father-in-law did a lovely waltz. The family had an invitation to 'a bit of a do', and I asked my father-in-law why he wasn't going. He told me that he had hung up his dancing shoes now. How visionary was he? Within a few days he was suddenly taken into hospital, his life hanging in the balance; I went with my mother-in-law to see him. When we came away she asked me if I would go to church with her to pray. Of course I did. While we did so, I looked up into the nave of the church and saw this enormous white stallion rearing up on its hind legs. I somehow knew that it was a symbol of his spirit trying to stay with my mother-in-law. He was really putting up a fight. Then an enormous hand - I took it to be God's - came and gathered the horse up and took it. I realised that dad was not going to win his battle, and he didn't. He was a young man by today's standards, only late fifties. For a long time his spirit was represented to me by a horse. My mother-in-law loved doves and kept seeing one in her garden for many years; she believed it was a sign of him. When she died I always seemed to have a pair of doves in my garden. Maybe this is fancy, I don't really know. A pair of doves are still here today and I am living in a different house nowadays.

Once my daughter Julie delved more into Spiritualism and started to try out her mediumship, she tried to give me a reading. I say tried because it is a recognised situation in this activity, that to give family or friends a true reading is difficult. Their backgrounds, family connections, hopes, desires and interests are usually known, so it is doubly hard. It is much, much easier when you do not know the person at all. Julie was in contact with my mother, her grandmother, and they were talking about my operation, my paintings and so on, things she also knew about, and my mother was giving reassurances about. Then suddenly she saw the image of my real biological father, whom even I do not know. Julie reported that he was just saying that he truly was my real father, when again out of the blue my father-in-law stood in front of him and said to her, "No, I'm her father now." When my father-in-law was alive, I had sort of adopted him as my dad too. He was a quiet man but with an occasional saucy kind of humour. When I first knew him I wasn't sure how to take him, but we got on well. I did have a harder time calling my mother-in-law 'Mum' because I already had mine. We had our differences but settled nicely after a time and we got on famously. So I do think Julie was tuning in to spirit very well.

My mother-in-law now comes back to tell mediums that I can call on her for help. Neither of my in-laws believed in spirit, although my mother-in-law believed in 'God, or something'. Just before she died, she told me about waking in the night and seeing two shining bright figures at the foot of her bed. One she took to be her husband and the other, who wore a hooded cloak which covered his face so she couldn't see him, she thought was God. All of her children and I were with her when she died. She had said that she wanted it this way, and at the very last moment she looked up and gave a big smile. I think her husband must have been there to greet her. Thinking and writing about this beautiful reunion has brought tears to my eyes. They had a great love for one another.

# In My View

This chapter is purely my own thoughts about Spiritualism and my personal beliefs. The really good thing about this religion is that you are free to think things out in your own way. My reasoning is that no-one should make a person believe the way they say. It is up to each soul to find its own path.

When I meet people who are trying to become mediums they are all afraid that what they are seeing is just their own imagination. You do have to believe that your own guides or helpers are aiding you. The interpretation of what you see can stray somewhat but generally you should say what you see, hear, feel or sense. Yes, you can get things wrong but you are only human. Other people including spiritualists have to realise that an individual must start somewhere. Perhaps one should put a large L sign on your torso. People please remember that the training period can take time and that the beginner is doing his or her best.

I do believe that everyone has psychic ability but they are not used to putting it into practice consciously. However, people do use it in some form or another, as my father-in-law did. How many times do people pick up the telephone and the person at the other end says, "I was just thinking about calling you"? There are times when you and someone else say the same thing together. That deja-vu feeling, but you know that you have never been to that particular place.

I have a very good friend of long-standing named Doris. She is particularly sensitive even though she does not really believe in Spiritualism, though she believes in God. We were going on a short holiday with our grown-up children and my granddaughter one year and we were looking forward to it. The day before we went, in the middle of packing, I was struck immobile by tremendous pain from my right hip to my toes. I couldn't move because of the pain. My husband called an ambulance and off I was carted to the local hospital. The doctors couldn't quite make out what had happened to cause this and so they admitted me. As I lay in pain in the A &E Department my friend bustled in. She was full of anxiety and searching for me. How did she know I was there? I have no idea other than spirit intervention. Later I asked her how she found me. Doris said that I hadn't called her to say that we were off like I usually do. But this was the day before I was due to go away. She said she had told her husband that she felt something was wrong but he thought that she was making a fuss over nothing. She had `phoned different hospitals until she tried this one and found that I had been admitted there. Doris came straight over and even bluffed her way into the A & E by telling them she was my sister. This is a bit of a laugh because we are nothing like each other. She is tall, slim and elegant, while I am of average height and a bit dumpy. I am sure that she had used her psychic ability naturally.

When she was young, my daughter kept bringing me baby birds that had fallen out of their nests. We never had much luck in keeping them alive, except for once, hence the poem.

## An Answered Prayer

*My daughter found a baby bird,*
*fallen from its nest,*
*tearfully she brought it me*
*for sustenance and rest.*

## IN MY VIEW

*I looked upon its soulful eyes,*
*it's feebleness of cry,*
*no feather warmed its red raw throat,*
*I was sure that it would die.*
*My heart just sank, for many times*
*she'd given me this stress,*
*and though together we would try,*
*we never had success.*
*That night I prayed to our good Lord,*
*"Why send me creatures small,*
*to succour and to keep alive?*
*I am no good at all."*
*In tears I prayed that just this once*
*this wretched bird would live,*
*for though I had no hope for it,*
*I gave all that I could give.*
*A week then passed and, to our joy,*
*he grew better every day;*
*with shaky flight around the room,*
*he would soon be on his way.*
*We let him go, with feelings mixed,*
*in our garden there;*
*silently I thanked the Lord*
*for answering my prayer.*

I firmly believe in the power of prayer. I always have a list in my head of people, friends and family who need healing and I do my absent healing prayer for them. Not necessarily in church, but anywhere that I happen to be. In the garden is my favourite place. If I know where the problem is, I go inside the body to try and break up the bad matter and then heal afterwards. I have got a fair idea of how the body looks on the inside as I once did an O Level in Human Biology and I am interested. I do pray also for the health and wellbeing of this beautiful planet of ours. In my talks with God I ask him not to let us ruin all this beauty. A dutiful father does guide his family and sometimes restricts their actions. I do understand about free will, but I ask Him please to not let us destroy this lovely place.

My son, who tried healing at first, told me about an individual who came to him for prayer and healing, which he did, but then went home and died. He felt so terrible about the experience that he almost gave up. However he now thinks of it as easing the path to the other side.

# Dreams and Visits

At one time I was visited by the spirit of a very old man. I could see him everywhere, in the room, in the streets, and in my dreams. In dreams he took me to a large room with many other elderly men. They all wore long black, loose flowing robes with a flattish hat. Their faces were lined and they had very, very long beards. In this room there were stands like lecterns but much longer, with large tomes on them. He opened one and showed me what was written inside. I can remember being fascinated by the books but unfortunately I never could remember what was written inside. It was most frustrating.

Many years later, in dream state, I met Vincent Van Gough. I must add here that I also paint. I use many media, water colour, oils, pastel and such. I also do clay work and luckily had a piece exhibited in the Royal Academy. However at this particular time I had been looking at Van Gough and his life and sympathising with his problems, vaguely wondering what would have resulted if things had happened differently. If he had married, would he have had a happier life? If he had any children of his own, would he have been less dedicated to his art and maybe not disturbed in his mind? But then we may not have had the pleasure of seeing so much of his art, as consequently he may not then have painted so much.

In my dream I was by the side of the Seine. Van Gough came to the scene by bike, which he rested against a wall, and together he and I walked along the banks. He spoke to me about his work, explaining his ideas and technique and I understood everything. Again though, when I awoke I could not remember. Oh bother, bother, bother!

## To Van Gogh

*What vivid colours spring to the eye,*
*streaks and swirls do paint the parts,*
*the substance and the texture lay*
*displaying all his visual arts.*

*I read about the man, his way of life,*
*sorrow rose for unrequited passion;*
*if only love had found for him a wife,*
*would the story then be of different fashion.*

*Dreaming, there beside the Seine he stood,*
*leaned his bike against a wall just near,*
*he walked and taught me so I understood*
*the meaning of his art was clear.*

*I woke trying to recall, what did he say?*
*He spoke to me in such a friendly tone,*
*but like a distant mist all fades away,*
*alas he is gone, and I am left alone.*

*Yet still my heart stirs with 'The Cypress Tree',*
*shines with 'The Starry Sky' at night,*
*it bobs with boats in 'Saint Marie',*
*turning my darkness into light.*

## DREAMS AND VISITS

While I am on the subject of dreams, I must say here that I do not believe that every dream has some relevant meaning to the dreamer. I think that it is a mixture of things, such as experiences you have had, in your life or through that day. You may dream of things that you have seen or people that you meet and talk to, often all mixed and jumbled up. Terrors or fears and phobias can end up with a related nightmare. Spiders are often in my dreams when I am anxious or worried because I do have a phobia about them. However I do believe that we astral journey at times. You instinctively know when you have been on a journey.

My mother was not a well woman for most of her life. She had suffered from TB and bronchitis as well as mental problems. She used to go to a group of doctors in our surgery. I related very well to a couple of doctors there. During a conversation, one of them came to realise that she was my mother. He confessed to me that when he saw her in the surgery he prayed that she was not coming to see him. It appears that she predicted that his wife was pregnant and that the baby was not going to touch this world. He was very nervous because it was true that his wife was pregnant and that she was having difficulties with the baby at that time. My mother would never have said this sort of thing normally. Her mental ability at that time was unbalanced. As it happens, all was fine in the end. He urged me to have her committed but I said "No." How could I, when I believed in the same power of spirit as she did. When Mum recovered I told her the story and she was upset that she did this prediction but glad that I did not have her committed, as it was all electric shock treatment then.

The night my mother died I had a curious dream about a duck bobbing about in a dirty barrel of water. Standing beside it was another barrel of perfectly clean, clear water. The duck flew out of the dirty barrel and into the clean one and started to preen itself. It was happy as it dunked its wings and swam up and down. It was my habit to go into my mother on the way to work and make her breakfast, and then pop in again on the way home. As I went in the next morning after the dream I found her in bed and her spirit had gone. I felt her pulse and talked to her. As I touched her I remember thinking that this is now just a shell. Our bodies really are just a vehicle for the spirit or soul. I feel that this dream represented her leaving this world, which was the barrel of dirty water, and going to the next by flying to the clean water where she was cleansed. Why I interpret this dream as her passing is that she told me once that her big brother was tall and handsome when he was young and her sister was considered a beauty so she thought that she was the ugly duckling. In my view she was no such thing. She had beautiful brown twinkling eyes. My mother was also a kind and sympathetic woman who would give you her last penny if you asked her. When I think of what she gave up to keep me, when in those days women who had babies out of wedlock were locked up or were forced to give their babies up for adoption. She must have had a hard time. Together we had hard times, but that's another story.

Apart from dreams you can also travel during meditation. I have had some beautiful and fascinating journeys in meditation. I was having a Reiki treatment by my very good friend and neighbour, Sharon. While I went into a meditational state of mind I saw the most beautiful North American shawl with a tapestry border. This border, of pattern and people, moved along the edge of the shawl in a most fascinating manner, creating a wonderful sight and warmth. I would never have even imagined something like this. It was a unique experience. I would love to have it again. Unfortunately the next Reiki session I had I was violently sick and Sharon has been wary about repeating the experience.

I have also had some terrifying dreams and nightmares of which I am not sure about. One dream was set in a windmill and I wrote this poem about the nightmare.

DREAMS AND VISITS

# The Nightmare

*Blackness surrounds a threatening air,*
*something pulses, something stirs,*
*a windmill's sails go slowly round,*
*a safe haven I have found.*
*I climb the winding stairs to the top,*
*see an exhibition about the crop;*
*at ease I stop and look about,*
*then a hulking form begins to shout.*
*A gleaming axe he raises high,*
*I cannot run although I try,*
*about me lay all chopped off limbs*
*and blood is splattered over things.*
*My heart now beats a faster drum,*
*a voice within my ear cries, "Run."*
*I blindly stumble to the stairs,*
*my eyes are wild and full of tears,*
*round and round I run, yet find*
*his breath is growing close behind.*
*I chance a glance at my pursuer,*
*emitting the stink of a foul sewer,*
*an evil aura swirls, green then red,*
*and blacken where his wounds have bled.*
*I tumble, fall, let out a scream,*
*it rides the night although a dream.*

I did not wake, which is usual in these types of dreams, but for me quite often there has been a 'saviour'. After this one, I was suddenly out in space floating besides an enormous cross. I can only describe this in a comparison: I was like a microbe on the skin of a giant. The cross of Christ was lit by millions of white bulbs and all around me I heard the Heavenly choir singing Ave Maria. It was sung by thou-

# THE NARROW DOORWAY

sands of angels, I just knew, and it was the most beautiful singing I have ever heard. I really cannot put into words the utmost beauty of this experience. However another 'saviour' was just a voice singing merrily, 'When Irish eyes are smiling,' and I smiled and sang along with it.

In another dream, I was with an older gentleman along with Sharon. We were walking by a river. We intended to go fishing and he was teaching us. I'll add here that I do not fish nor had I any ambition to. On a hill was the club house and on the other side of the river there was an island which you could get to by crossing a small bridge. Further along, by a bend in the flow, there stood a small infants' school and I could hear their childish voices at play. I had a small chair with me, as in real time I have back trouble, and I went to put it on the bank but decided that in the little mud there my chair would sink, so I chose another site. Sharon continued walking and talking with the man.

Now why do I think this was a little bit of Heaven? The colours there were magnificent. The greens of the grass and trees were greener, the blue of the sky and the white clouds, and most convincing of all was that the air I was breathing was so light, so sweet; I have never breathed air like this before. Most ordinary dreams you forget or can't quite remember; it's the special ones that you remember for life.

# Like-Minded People

Spiritual churches are wonderful places to go and meet kindred souls who share your views and ways of thinking about how you should live your life and what to expect in the next. Once in a local church the medium gave the service and her messages to a few people there, but I had the impression of fire and a danger to her. At the end of the service I went up to her and said that I thought she should be careful around flammable things. She said that her aunt had a fire in her house and that it was probably that but everything was alright now. I said "Fine" and went to move away. However, I was not comfortable with this explanation; then spirit told me that this was not what it meant and it was more to do with her personally. I felt worried about her safety and so I approached her again and said that I was sorry but I had been told that it wasn't about her aunt, it was for her. Then she confessed that she had already been badly burnt on her arms and upper body and she was recovering well. I then realised that it was a past condition I was picking up on but I was glad that I went back to her.

My local church is called the Beacon of Light, situated in north London. It is a warm church full of warm people who will go out of their way to help anyone if they can. There are times when I have been sitting in the congregation that I see spirits around but I do not know who they are there for. Sometimes the medium will also see them and direct them to the right person so that I know I have seen correctly. There are many times when I do not get confirmation though. Very often I am looking at the medium and concentrating on what they are saying and then see something that may be for them. However I cannot keep going up to them after the meeting to tell them because it seems too pushy. Other times they are whisked off to the back room for a cuppa.

At odd times, if I have been to an art course or some other residential or day course, the conversation has somehow got around to beliefs of mine and others. I often end up trying to do a reading for somebody. I was in one such situation and I had contacted this lady's grandmother. She was very small and very neat person but such a fierce and strong character. I can see her now in my mind's eye. She had white hair, done in a swept up style. Her clothes were black and high at the neck with a little white lace showing. She looked about late seventy to eighty years old. As she was telling me what to say, she uttered a word I have never heard. I can't remember now what it was, but I was reluctant to come out with it. She became very angry with me telling me "Go on, you say it to her" in a most bullying manner. So I did repeat it, saying I was sorry that I didn't know why I had to tell her this but I was ordered to do so. The lady listened to me and then gave a big smile. She told me that it was a name that she and her siblings had called their grandmother, a silly name that really had no meaning. It goes to show that you must say what spirit tell you because although it is nonsense to you it means something to the concerned person and I learned a lesson on that day.

At one time I was on the committee of our local art group and our chairman was not well at all. After about a year he died; I went to his funeral and met his wife whom I had seen at our annual dinner but had never really spoken to. Just after the funeral I was mopping the kitchen floor when he came to me and put the idea of sending his wife some flowers. I thought about this and decided that the

# LIKE-MINDED PEOPLE

flowers sent on that sad day are just left there and it might be nice to have some in the house. So I went out and purchased some and arranged to have them sent to her home. The next day she rang and thanked me. This seemed fine to me but alas it wasn't for him. He kept saying, "They're not from you, they're from me, tell her that." He would not let me get on with my housework, just kept saying they were from him. I dutifully rang her back and said a little about my faith, because all this could have been confusing for her. I told her that he wanted me to tell her that the flowers were from him. I do think she thought I was a bit weird, but she took it well.

A couple of weeks later he came back to me and said that - he gave me a couple of names - were not taking his death well, one of them exceptionally hard. He wanted to tell them he was fine. I didn't really want to 'phone her again but I did and asked if we could meet to talk. I thought it might be easier this way. We made a date but she later cancelled it as she was very unsure of me. So I never did get that final message over. I do see her now and again but I say nothing of spirit, just chatter casually.

Two of my grandsons had started up a trio with a friend I shall called Ted. They were in their last year at school. One played the drums and the other two played guitars. They were doing very well and had played a few gigs locally. One of my grandsons had won a competition for an original song, but mostly Ted wrote and the others put their bit in. They had been invited to play at the Hertfordshire Schools' Gala at the Royal Albert Hall. They accepted and we were all excited about going to see them. The very next day after they had accepted, Ted died in a car accident. A friend who had just passed her driving test had invited him and three others to go out at dinner break to get something to eat. Ted was the only one who died. Of course, my grandsons were badly affected by this. They were among his pallbearers. They also said that they couldn't play at the Albert Hall because Ted was no longer there. Eventually they decided to do it; they left the drums out and both played acoustic

# THE NARROW DOORWAY

guitar. They chose three of Ted's songs to sing. I felt the management there were brilliant. They blew up an enormous photo of Ted as a backdrop and his family had the most prestigious box. Someone came to tell the story of what had happened to Ted and how the boys were dedicating the evening to him. We were all very proud of them.

A short while after, I was sitting and thinking of Ted when he came and said, "Tell them I'm okay." I replied that I would have to tell them more than that, as they would think it's just their odd old grandmother talking. I'll add here that they do know about my beliefs and spiritual matters as their mother and uncle are both excellent mediums. Anyway, Ted just said one word: "Discombobulate." I didn't understand and thought I had heard incorrectly, so I tried to get him back. However he didn't return. He didn't tell me but I had the impression that he was trying to put the word into one of his songs.

When I told the boys about this visit and I tried to repeat the word, but I said that I wasn't sure about it. My grandsons and my daughter smiled and told me that they knew what it was. It seems that he regularly found extraordinary words and tried to get them into use around the school, also that he was trying to work it into a song. I was so pleased that I had spoken to him and that he had given me something the boys would recognise and not something I had made up. There was no way I could have known that. I looked it up in the dictionary and it means 'to throw into confusion'. It certainly did that to me.

# Spirit Guides

Everyone has spirit guides who are with you for all of your life. Others may come and go depending on your needs at certain times. They do not make decisions for you, but give you support for whatever path you take.

I had been told by a medium, a long time ago, that I had a French nun for a spirit guide. I could well imagine that this guide would be given to me to help with calmness as I had no patience and a quick temper when I was young. However I had never seen her or spoken to her. This changed as I grew much older and she did make herself known to me just once. I was learning how to meditate with a friend and teacher, when she suddenly came. I asked her why she hadn't talked to me before. She replied that it wasn't the right time and I had not been ready for her, but it will come later. Unfortunately I haven't seen or heard from her again.

I was also told that I have a Native American Indian guide. I have a great interest in the people and their traditional way of life, and also with the ancient Egyptian gods and belief system, but I really haven't had any actual contact with them. Once I did go to Egypt, and, as I sat by the Sacred Lake, I tried to go back in time to see if I had been there in the past. As far as I could tell I never had, but whether this is because I had lost the ability to go into my past lives or not, I am uncertain.

# THE NARROW DOORWAY

I know that I have spirit guides in my life, because they have 'saved' me a few times. However guides in your life do change sometimes. The first time I was saved was when I was about nine years of age. I was coming home from school with a younger friend and I was sucking a large gobstopper. As I sucked hard it shot down my throat and stuck there. I was coughing and choking, and couldn't breathe. I tried to indicate to my friend to slap me on my back but he didn't understand. Suddenly a stranger came and hit my back hard and the sweet popped out. Now I didn't know whether my saviour was a man or a woman as he or she had disappeared. Usually with a child, you stop and ask them if they are alright or if they have far to go, or something. Whoever this was saved my life. Was it a guardian angel? I'll probably never know for sure.

The second time, which was recently, my saviour informed my husband about a situation. I had many sleepless and painful nights due to my legs, even after taking drugs. This particular night at about four o'clock in the morning I had given up trying to sleep in my bed and got up to sit in an armchair downstairs. I got a blanket and put the fire on to warm the room and settled down to try and sleep there. My husband said that he was woken by a woman - whom he took to be me in his sleepy state - who came into the room and told him to get up as he was needed. He stumbled around different rooms looking for me. When he found me I was sitting up straight with my head falling forward fast asleep. However the blanket edge was dangerously near to the gas fire flames and he moved it away.

When I woke up I saw him sitting on the settee watching me. He then asked me if I had come into the bedroom to wake him up. I replied that I hadn't been in to him at all. He was definitely sure that 'someone' had. Was I in danger? I could have been, but someone up there likes me, and considering my husband does not believe in spirit and life after death, I think this is amazing.

At the very beginning of the social interaction of mankind, probably in the early Stone Age, people believed in some kind of force for

# SPIRIT GUIDES

good and bad. The good brought you success in hunting and in finding food. It also brought you children to love and to help the clan or tribe. So a group of people living together would have good hunters or fishermen. Other members of the group were probably given the responsibility of finding berries, fruit and roots to eat. Maybe certain people did the cooking when fire first came into use. There would have been some organization occurring.

Very often in this kind of group there would have been a medicine man or woman, who would have developed some knowledge about the use of herbs and plant life that could help to heal people when they were sick or caught a disease or sustained wounds. The medicine man or woman would have used some implements and prayers to aid the healing process, also to drive away any negative forces. They may have said incantations only known to them and handed down through time. This would have given them great power and esteem in the eyes of the tribe members. This formation of groups happened without any knowledge of one another. This type of person was to be known as the shaman. Even at the beginning of social interaction there was an acknowledgement of something beyond this world. We can look at early cave paintings of animals and people going about their daily lives and the evidence of how they buried their dead, thus gain an insight to the way early man thought and the beliefs that they apparently had.

Voltaire once said, "If there were no God, it would have been necessary to invent one." I think that I agree with him.

In this poem I have used the cave painter in the role of the shaman, and as the intermediary between people and God, or many gods and spirits. Think of the awe and wonder early man must have had when they found that they could make marks and pictures with a likeness of life around them. They might have thought it imbued power and honour to the person who could create an image that lasted in this way.

33

# When the World was Young

*The young I entered the grey-walled cave,*
*knuckles trailing the dusty floor,*
*one finger picked up some red powder,*
*one spit to clear, and a rub on the wall*
*left a smear, deep as the setting sun*
*at the close of wake-time*
*that spread pale across the sky,*
*gradually fading,*
*amazing.*

*The older I gather the red sun,*
*my clan shows me great respect*
*because of my red cave marks.*
*I honour the gods with our lives on the wall,*
*for they give us all we need.*
*We are hungry, they give us food,*
*thirsty, they show us the way to water,*
*fur clothing,*
*warming.*

*The dying I lies in the grey-walled cave,*
*surrounded by our four-footed prey,*
*I enter my last deep red death pass,*
*a god, hunted, his blood life trickling away,*
*as mine is also fading.*
*In my grey haze I spy the hunters gathering,*
*running and chasing, in the gods' hereafter;*
*they are calling me, summoning,*
*coming.*

## SPIRIT GUIDES

I do know a terrific teacher and worker with the shamans of the various Indian tribes. His name is Les Fuller. He often does workshops with a group of people to open their awareness to healing, rebirths and animal guides. I have often attended these workshops and have been on wonderful journeys with his guidance. In one however I did an unfortunate prediction in symbolic form. I meditated and went on a journey and saw the most enormous turtle swimming in the sea. It was battling with the waves and then a very large wave turned it upside down. We have a saying, 'to turn turtle.' Les helped me by giving me interpretations of the symbols. They foretold that a ship would be overturned by an enormous wave, and quite soon. About two to three days later this actually happened and many lives were lost. It is a terrible thing to have such a prediction come true and somehow I kept feeling that I was responsible. I did have tears in my eyes when I heard. He was very good at reasoning with me, saying that I had in no way influenced this event.

One other time years before this, I was dancing with my husband in our bowls club when I caught sight of a couple also dancing who were our friends, named Frank and Margaret. I stopped and asked them if they did the pools. They answered "Yes." I said that they mustn't stop doing them as they were going to have a small win. They asked when this was going to happen and I thought for a moment, then replied it would be March the following year. I emphasized that it was a very small win. Where all this came from I have no idea. Life continued as usual and, the following March, Margaret told me that she thought of this prediction on the eve of the last day of the month and thought, 'Well, only one more day in March left.' The next day in the post was news of a small win. This was a lovely happy prediction.

Another remarkable occurrence that happened recently in the workshop was to do with healing. A woman who was with the group needed some healing on her neck. Part of the process was calling on the skills of 'spider spirit' to help repair the damage. As I have mentioned I have a problem with spiders so I was not entirely at ease with this. In my naivety I thought that I'd make a pretence of this. However what happened was no pretence. I opened my hand and held it in front of me and almost immediately a rather large tarantula sat in it. 'Oh,' I thought, 'why couldn't it have been a money spider, that I could cope with.' We were instructed to place the spider on the woman's bent neck, which I did as soon as I could, just to get rid of it. As I placed it, the spider stung me on my little finger and I jumped and shook my hand. At the same time it stung the woman, because she turned to me and inquired whether I had just put a spider on. She had felt the sting go through the back of her neck to the front. It did hurt for quite ten minutes after. Now I don't believe that the tarantula bit her or me, but this type of spider has stinging hairs on its legs which it sheds when it thinks it is in danger. I think I frightened it as much as it frightened me. Les however said that it was a good sign for it meant that the spider was sharing its power and strength with me. One had done the same with him and he also has a problem with spiders.

# Thoughtful Readings

When I do a reading for anyone, I do see what may be relevant to the inquirer or a trend of things as well as places and people in their past and present life. Might I add here that there is a great responsibility on the reader's behalf to handle the readings with the utmost care and consideration for the person they are with. You cannot blurt out dire information without some gentleness and thought in your approach. I try to smooth the pathway to any difficult situation. I have heard about many people set worrying and grief-stricken when careless mediums have handled readings without any thought. I have even heard of mediums saying that people should get divorced or separated, or a friendship to end on their say-so. I do not believe that this is the medium's job. The medium, according to the Spiritualists' National Union, is to offer proof of an existence of life after death. People must be free to make their own decisions.

There are poor mediums out there and of course fake ones, just like there are poor teachers, fake doctors and so on. However there are good and excellent ones too. A good idea is to go by word of mouth, or visit your local Spiritualist church and gain information there. Spiritualist churches are around, usually tucked away in some small place that gets overlooked. If you are unsure, go online to find your local one. Churches are lovely just to sit and find some inner peace; the people accept you without knowing or caring about your religious beliefs. There may be Catholics, Protestants and Jews, plus atheists, and probably many more within the movement.

Colour is very important to me. I first became aware of beautiful colour after the flat was bombed. Mum and I were moved between colourless old buildings, whose interiors looked frightening to me. However, one day we were moved into an American shelter to a small twin-bedded room. Over the beds spread beautiful patchwork quilts of all bright and cheerful colours and patterns. I loved them. Since then, I have always noticed colour. I hope to take a few students soon to help them perceive their feelings about colour and how to use them when reading for others.

As I have already stated I do believe in the power of prayer, whether in church or out. Prayer is potent anywhere on this planet. My grandson was trying to find a job after he had finished university and was beginning to despair. He was willing to take anything. I told him, via email, to ask the angels and his guides for help. He emailed back and asked, 'How do I do that, Nan?' which made me smile. I replied to just pray for help. Within two weeks he had obtained some work; it was only in a warehouse but it paid the bills. He returned home and was lucky to find another position, so it all added up on his CV.

I often call on my guides or angels when I fear some difficulty in life. I am not good at parking my car and need a lot of space so I quietly say to my angels, "Please help me find a good place to park." More often than not I do find one. When I'm driving through thunder and lightning and the roads can become slippery, I ask for safety. A call on them when I am going into hospital eases my mind, and so on. Do try calling on the angels when you have a need, and they will help you as much as they can.

# THOUGHTFUL READINGS

# Dear Lord

*Dear Lord,*
*my family, will you please bless,*
*with health and strength and happiness,*
*so they may live upon this Earth*
*in peace, with thankfulness and worth.*

*Dear Lord,*
*for those ill or weary, far from calm,*
*I ask for them a healing palm.*
*Please let them feel your gentle care,*
*that they may smile and know you're there.*

*Dear Lord,*
*for all the creatures you've placed here,*
*let them be loved and have no fear,*
*for all the creatures on the wing,*
*let them rejoice, your praises sing.*

*Dear Lord,*
*just one moment more I pray,*
*to look upon myself today;*
*please judge my heart by what you see,*
*and bear in mind my own mortality.*

I would like to approach the subject of reincarnation. Many think that this is not what happens for us, others think the opposite. Some people believe that you can be born again in the form of an animal, bird or insect, and live their lives by the thought that one day it could be them. I wonder, if this is the case, whether you are aware of yourself in that particular form of life? Many people believe they will rise again when the last trumpet is sounded by God. There are probably many more beliefs that I am not aware of. However I personally believe that we are reborn again as a human being, either as a man or woman. When we die, our spirit leaves the shell of our body and goes towards 'the light of God'. I believe in many levels within this light and that your soul or spirit goes to a level appropriate to the way you have lived your life. At whichever level you attain, you are able to look back upon your life and see the mistakes that you have made. Once recognised you must go through a learning procedure. For example, let's presume you have been unkind to many people in your life on Earth: learning different ways of handling kindness in thought and deed would be open for you. I have put this in a very simplistic form but it demonstrates a thought.

At one time I had a recurring dream about tsunami waves. These dreams were vivid and disturbing and try as I might I could not think why I should suddenly start dreaming of them. At that time, tsunamis were not talked about much or reported in the news. I lived not far from the Thames, by Tower Bridge,, and would often push my daughter in her pram there to watch the river traffic.

In one dream, the flood was approaching and I thought that I would turn my wardrobe onto its back and put my children inside to float. A mother who lived in the flat below said to me that this was a good idea and asked if she could put her children in. I felt in my dream that her children would make the weight too much and it would sink, so I said to her to do the same with her own wardrobe. Next, I remember wondering whether I should head down to the river where possibly a boat would pick us up, or go the opposite way to higher ground, as though this were all feasible in real life.

Dreams of this nature plagued me every night. Somehow I began to realise that this is what happened to me in a former life. I suddenly had a memory of being a young boy about fifteen years of age. I saw myself as this lad wearing a toga and running up a road shouting to people that a wave was coming. I was rushing towards a building that had Roman type columns outside, but I never reached the

# THOUGHTFUL READINGS

building and everything went black. I do believe that I was in Atlantis because the wave looked a mile high, it was enormous. After I realised what these dreams were about, I stopped having them, much to my relief. I do though get very uneasy and frightened when I read about them, or see them on television. They seem to happen more frequently nowadays.

Another time I remembered fainting, as if it were a memory in this life. I was trying to think when this happened. I pondered over the memory and decided that I have never fainted in this life. Then I sort of day-dreamed, it's the only way to describe it, and saw myself as a woman in rough attire of almost a full length dress and apron with a bonnet and a wooden yolk across my shoulders that carried milk. I was by St Martin-in-the-Fields, Trafalgar Square, on the street that runs by the side of it. I experienced a great pain in my leg and fainted there. Someone helped me up and took me to a 'hospital' that lay to the back of that church. I must have fainted again because when I woke I was lying on my back on a sort of raised plank of wood. That hospital is not there now but I did wonder if it were the beginning of Charing Cross Hospital not far away. By looking on the Internet I have tried to establish some facts to consolidate this, though nothing exact has come up. What I have discovered is that there used to be alms houses at the back of St Martin-in-the-Fields. The Greek word for alms houses is 'hositium', from which our word hospital comes. Also, in 1697 a dispensary movement opened. There were three in London and one of them was in St Martin's Lane, which runs by the church. In these dispensaries they would give free advice to anyone who wished for it. So the vision I had could well have a sound basis. I also found a lot of information, besides interesting reading, in a book called 'The Evolution of Hospitals in Britain' (published by Poynter).

Now in this life I have always had trouble with my legs and feet, and have pain in them. It all stemmed from a spinal condition and

# THE NARROW DOORWAY

this increased later in life to a much greater degree. I have spent years in an old-fashioned corset and had many visits to osteopaths. In the end, though, I had three minor and two major operations and one more to come. I wonder if this is related to a past life.

I began to get the knack of casting my mind backwards. I have remembered three other lives. In one I was a Frenchman, a gaoler in the dungeons of a castle. I was utterly vile, dirty and wicked. This life consisted of violence, bribery, rape and in every way I could I tried to take advantage of my meagre position. I try not to think of him much.

In another life I was totally the opposite, a gentle and mild man who worked in the fields for the lord of that area and with a small patch for my own needs. I was forced to go to war by this lord when I was needed. I saw myself marching with others and I was thinking that all I wanted to do was to return to my wife and family whom I loved dearly. This character was killed on the battlefield by a lance that pierced him. This seemed to be happening in the Norman times.

The final life was set in China. I was the daughter of a high official and lived in the ideal surroundings of a typical Chinese house set within a beautiful garden. I saw the back of myself on a veranda looking at my father. I loved him very much. The love he sent out to me was so very much it overwhelmed me and I started to cry. The Emperor's name or dynasty was Chiang. I did try to follow this up on the Internet and found something akin to that name. Apart from the St Martin life, these lifetimes have nothing that I can pick up on and research unfortunately.

I know about these five and no more, and now I have lost the ability to cast my mind back. It seemed available to me for only a few years. However I do believe we are put into certain circumstances to live a different type of life in which to learn whatever we must, to enable us to reach a higher level.

# Mum as She Grew Older

As my mother grew older and unable to manage as she used to, I found her a flat in a communal house with an aide to come and help her if she needed anything, plus a nurse to help her with a bath. My family was out all day working and I had not long started a new career in teaching and was out a lot. As I have mentioned already I would make her breakfast in the morning. One day I went in asking her to tell me what she wanted quickly as I was running late. I received no reply so I went to her bed and found her dead. The shock was tremendous. She had been ill for many years and in your heart you know it has to happen but nothing really prepares you for it.

Time passes and about six months later my husband and I were driving down to Devon for a holiday. When he drives he doesn't talk much and I sat gazing out of the window. I must have gone into a trance state but at the time did not realise it. I heard a telephone ringing in my left ear. 'Pick the `phone up, one of you,' - meaning one of my children - I thought. No-one did so I thought I'd better pick it up. I heard an organ playing 'Oh You Beautiful Doll'. Mentally I asked who was there and my mother answered saying, "Me of course." My mother could play the organ and had often sung this song to me. "Hello Mum," I replied, "What are you doing?" She didn't say much, only that it wouldn't be long. She kept repeating that it wouldn't be long. "What won't be long?" I asked her. Mum replied that she wasn't allowed to tell me as He wouldn't allow it. I don't know how I knew it was God she was talking about; I just knew that the He had a capital letter.

I spent all that holiday thinking that I was going to die and see her again. I was tremendously cautious when walking on the cliff tops or going on a boat trip! I was on edge the whole time. Once, I sat on the edge of a cliff top to try and do some painting, expecting the cliff to give way and to go tumbling down. It was if I were thinking, 'Well, here is the opportunity to take me if you want to.' My husband went off for a walk and when he came back he had to help me up because I was frozen into that position and had a terrible headache.

While staying at the hotel we went for a walk around the grounds and came to a small bridge crossing a stream. I decided that this was a lovely place to take a photograph. I took one of my husband and he one of me. Another couple walking by offered to take a photograph of the two of us together, which I accepted. We took a lot of photos on that holiday and on getting them developed we found that in the picture of the two of us standing on this bridge there was a bright burning spot on my left leg. I had a lot of trouble with this one. None of the other photographs had this odd-looking burn. We returned home without any mishap and I thought, 'Well, nothing major occurred, I am still here so what was it all about?'

A few days later I woke in the middle of the night with a whirring sound in my ear. I was motionless; I don't remember even trying to move but I don't think I could have. The whirring seemed to be centred round my left hip. A circle spun around me. It began to spin so fast I felt that I was being drawn up into the air by my hip. I didn't go up but it felt as if I could and I was expecting to. The whirring noise was getting louder all the time. Then, suddenly, it all stopped and immediately I was asleep. I awoke the next morning with full knowledge of what went on during the night.

It then dawned on me what my mother was trying to say to me. She was a great believer in healing and did healing with many of her friends. When she was ill, towards the end of her life, she went constantly to healing sessions at her church. In fact, she would only go to healing and not to the doctor. I persuaded her to go in the end by saying that she should go to both as they both could help her. Anyhow, I knew then that she had been working to bring me healing and this is what she was excited about. She had brought some 'psychic surgeons' to me. From that moment on, the leg felt so much better. My toes, which were starting to curl under my feet, became straighter and not so painful. This helped me for many years. Thank you, Mum, and spirit. I'm a great believer in saying 'Thank you' to spirit, be it God, angels, guides or friends and family, when your prayers have been heard.

I always seemed to have had some pain from about the age of twenty, but I had a good run and managed to deal with it for a long time without the need of surgery. I had always been very nervous about operations on the spine because of the delicate nerves which run the length of it. However, once I reached a certain age I met a surgeon whom I immediately knew I could trust. It was a spiritual connection, I'm sure. I think I had been waiting to meet him through the years.

# Many Questions

*Why me, what am I, why am I here?*
*I possess the usual attributes of a human,*
*head, trunk and limbs, the mechanics of being,*
*a heart that pumps, lungs that go in and out,*
*the usual internal workings, no different from the next being.*
*Yet we are not alike in look or thought,*
*each is unique.*
*In some hazy distant time,*
*did I begin in some warm slick of mud?*
*Did God fashion the soul giving it life?*

## THE NARROW DOORWAY

*Or did some visitor from beyond*
*plant unearthly seeds, stand back and watch?*
*Well, here I am, not the finished item you understand,*
*I am just a sub-plot in development,*
*in a long line of sub-plots,*
*from past where to future there.*
*Will I appear again somewhere in time?*
*A body looking very much the same,*
*but it can't be me, can it?*
*Ah, but what about the soul, I feel I have one,*
*where it lies I cannot say for sure;*
*do souls ascend to a mythical Heaven or Hell?*
*Is one man's Heaven another man's Hell?*
*Who can tell?*

# So Many Questions

Like most people I have had my questions, especially when there was so much in the media about life on Earth started by aliens. So many people worldwide saying they have seen UFOs and others talking about being abducted. Then there's Darwin's evolution theory, all sounding very reasonable versus God and divine creation. It is very confusing to many who are not of a definite faith. In an attempt to come to some kind of settlement in my mind, I dismissed the UFOs, for by definition we do not know what they are, at least for the moment; though I would like to know and what it was that I saw many years ago.

My own faith is strongly on the side of God, not as an old man with a long beard, but as a great power for love and goodness. I also believe that everything has an opposite - black/white, up/down, in/out and so on – so then I must believe that the opposite of love is hate and the opposite of good is bad. If God stands for love then there must be an opposite, the power for hate, which we may call Satan. I can and have seen his power at work in the world and in my own life. Therefore I tend to merge the Darwin theory with God in the miracle of Earth.

God made the world in seven days, the Bible tells us. Well, how long is God's day? It could be centuries for all we know. Perhaps it was His will that life grew gradually in the way that Darwin suggested.

# THE NARROW DOORWAY

Then the story of the Garden of Eden could well be when God made a human soul to occupy the form: to give that pair free will and a choice of living their own way, and to understand that by making those choices they have to live with whatever comes after. If it were not that I have seen and heard spirit in my life, as do others, my choice would be difficult. As it is, my choice is made easy; God exists. My mother told me, before and after death, that He exists and proof has been sent to me.

One curious tale I can tell, though have no actual proof of as yet, is about Anglesey Abbey. It lies just beyond Cambridge and is open to the public all the year round. I usually visit once a year. Within the grounds of this abbey lies a walkway in the form of a massive cross, lined either side by trees and bushes. Where the path crosses the main walkway lies another narrower walk, lined with trees that have been encouraged to form the shape of an arch such as those in a church. I have been told that the monks who once lived there walked the length in contemplation. It is not the prettiest part of the grounds in my opinion, but I love to walk down there.

One day, a few years ago, I was strolling down it with my husband talking and suddenly 'someone' stepped in beside me, walking along with us. I became aware of a monk and he started talking to me about his life. He had been a carpenter in a village nearby and his name had been Matthew. Once he had entered the Abbey life, he was renamed Dominic. He had a lovely nature, kind and generous and full of fun. He did not tell me this but I sensed it. He would help the villagers when he could. He carried on talking but to be honest I can't quite remember what was said exactly, only that I felt so comfortable with him by my side. On walking back, I sat on a fallen tree trunk by the edge of the church avenue of trees. I thought of him in his time here and vaguely wondered if he had rested there. Dominic laughed heartily and said I was an idiot (in a joking manner) and that the tree had not been down in his day. I had to laugh too as he was perfectly right, it was a silly thought. He was

# SO MANY QUESTIONS

such a lovely spirit that I didn't want to say goodbye when he left me at the end of the avenue. I wished I could take him home with me. For a few days after the visit I kept thinking of him and missing him.

The following year I went again, eager to sense him once more, but instead another monk came and walked with me. I inquired where Dominic was and was told that he had gone ahead. What that meant I was uncertain. Did it mean that he had gone to God, or was it just that he was further ahead of us in his walk? This monk was totally different. A rounder figure, a bit brusque in his manner, and he seemed much sterner and also a stickler for rules and regulations. I didn't quite catch his name, but he told me that he had a hand in planning stages of the abbey and of bringing it all about. He lived in the thirteenth century. He was very proud of this. I replied that this couldn't be right as the abbey was built in the fourteenth century. He became very indignant and said that the planning had taken place in the latter part of the thirteenth and stormed off. I had the feeling that I was very firmly put in my place. Oh well, you can't win them all. I have read up a little since, via the Internet, and found that the abbey was originally built by Augustinian canons between 1100 – 1135 AD. However, extra land was acquired from the village of Bottisham in 1279 AD, which is around the time that the second monk was talking about.

The last time I was there I took my friend Sharon with me, another psychic and very open to the spirit world, truly sensitive. I had told her about my experiences at the abbey and she was looking forward to the visit. However, we were having a laugh and a mess about and naturally I couldn't sense anything and nor could she. Sharon noted my disappointment and said that she would move away from me. She wandered off talking to my husband about spirit and although he doesn't really understand, as a non-believer, he appreciates my feelings and beliefs. This does not interfere at all in our relationship as we do allow each other our different ways.

As they moved off I did meet a very different kind of monk. I did not find out his name or much about him; the impression I received

49

was that he was extremely shy and very reticent about talking to people. I could just about see him hiding behind trees and peering out. He was so meek I wondered what he did within the abbey. It felt as if he went there for safety and spent his life very much in seclusion and prayer. I was not with him long and so re-joined my husband and friend. Sharon had looked my way and sensed that I was with someone, and wondered if his shyness was because she was there. She did sense many spirits around the grounds but didn't get into conversation with any particular one. I was disappointed for her, and for the fact that her not connecting with spirit did not back up my experiences. I had hoped that she would also meet Dominic.

Sharon and I had an invitation to go to a mutual friend's house for meditation and development. Tracy made us and a few other people welcome in her home. Candles burned and lights turned low with soft music in the background. In this atmosphere I could go into 'spiritual mode' quite quickly.

Beautiful scenes and strange people would enter in and out of my vision, but of course not everyone actually sees. Seeing spirit is called clairvoyance. Many psychics may sense happenings, people and animals; they pick up clues by the feeling of spirit within the person, and this is called clairsentience. Others may hear spirit talking, which is named clairaudience; these psychics hear sounds and speech by which they may interact with spirit. I tend to think that many mediums use all three, depending on what is presented to them from their guides or helpers. I generally work this way, using all that is presented to me. While beautiful to watch these vague dreamy journeys that meditation brings, the lesson to be learned is how to control and how to investigate a given message.

It was in one of these sessions that I met and spoke to a particular spirit, along with a few others. I asked him his name and who the message was for. This information was given to me and found to be correct. I asked where had he had lived and again relayed this which was confirmed, mainly by Tracy, although the message was for her young relation. His message was about the lonely state that she was in at that time, because no school place was available when she needed one; then she had gone in late after the others had formed their friendship groups and she felt left out, cut off and lonely, which her great-grandfather understood. I relayed some information to her from him. At one point I asked him what his job had been. He prevaricated a bit, ending up with 'jack-of-all-trades' doing odd jobs around. Then with a little laugh he told me that he used to be a poacher, at which I too laughed and relayed this final piece. Apart from the poaching, which I supposed was kept secret, the rest was verified. I took part in many of these gatherings and spoke to or saw spirit; unless you make notes it is very difficult to remember them.

Once while I was receiving healing I visualised a scene where the road wandered down the slope of a hill and wound around, passing a house that at one time had been a country pub. Outside was an old fashioned garden that's rarely seen today. At the end of the healing I asked about the vision I had received and was told that it was the family home.

# Haunting

I was on holiday some years ago and went on a ghost walk in an old mansion. It started about midnight and went on to about two in the morning. The guide was very serious about his work, making it as real as he possibly could. This was a little difficult as many were there to just have a giggle. I went 'just to see'. At the beginning of the tour, everything went along without much connection for me. Yes, there was an aura about, well evoked by the guide I thought, but towards the end we came to two rooms in which I did connect with spirit. The second side room went down a few steps into what was once a bedroom. I saw or felt, I'm not sure which, a woman in a long flowing nightgown lying exhausted on the stairs. It looked as if she were trying to mount them but couldn't make it.

She was terrified. The aura of horror that came from that room hit me and I took a step or two back behind another person so that I was shielded by him from the force. I felt so sorry for that poor woman. In the room where I was standing there was a massive fireplace and I could feel the heat of a fire, although I could not see one. The guide went on to finish the story that he was going through before I could pick up anything from this room. My thoughts were still lingering on the anguish of the woman. The guide told of the master of the house who often took young local women to his bed. He was known to be a ruthless man. The young lady whom I saw lying on the stairs and whom he had bedded had just given birth to his illegitimate child. It seemed unbelievable, so the story goes, that he had seized the child as soon as it was born and thrown it into the burning fire. If the story is an actual fact, how wretched and helpless must that young mother have felt. This is one of the most gruesome stories I have ever heard. If Hell exists in the traditional sense of the meaning, this man would surely be there.

## Internment

*"Listen to me", said the Devil,*
*placing his hand on my heart,*
*"the dark is waiting for you,*
*quiet and peaceful and set apart*
*in the twilight of unhallowed ground."*

*"Listen to me," said the Dark One,*
*placing his lips to my ear,*
*"hear the church bells' lonely toll,*
*it fills the soul with terrible fear,*
*increasing with the faint thud of earth."*

*"Watch for me," beseeched Beelzebub,*
*placing an icy gaze on my grey eyes,*
*"even in death there is some sort of life,*
*urging the bleached bones to rise*
*and dance in the cold flames."*

*"Touch your world," said Satan,*
*placing my hand on the enclosing pine,*
*nails scratched, snatching the gloom,*
*feeling his breath mingle with mine,*
*I cry out to the departing forms*
*as he welcomes me in.*

# THE NARROW DOORWAY

I shall lift the mood to a much lighter level! At another meeting in an old mansion, I went with my friend Sharon and my daughter Julie, with her friend, to a late night supper and tour of the house. The evening consisted of about four mediums who were leaders in various groups in which we would spend some time. My son was one of the leaders, for the section on divining. This could be done with a forked twig, a rod or by a spindle on a thread. As my group entered the room he showed us these different ways of working, with stories attending them. He said that he had hidden an object within the room and we could take a preferred divining tool and see if we could find it. The object would be wrapped in brown paper. The room was large with a few books on a shelf and statues and not much else but large heavy chairs. I tried out a spindle and a forked twig but alas I had no inkling where to go, nor did I feel anything in particular from holding them. My friend Sharon however did find it. There were long heavy drapes around the windows that went to the floor and the object, a spoon, was hidden there. She said that she could definitely feel the pull.

A camera and computer were set up in another room, capable of spotting orbs within the room right at that moment. My daughter Julie, who works with computers a lot, did not really trust it as she knew what can be manipulated on a computer. It was fascinating, but again I did not feel or sense anything in particular.

But one of the two places that I did sense something was down in the cellars. It was very cold down there and with only a low wattage bulb it felt odd. We stood in a row on one side of the cellar while the leader told us that he was going to turn the light off so that we were in total darkness, but if anyone felt they desperately needed the light turned back on, they should speak up. Now, the idea that this was going to be a serious course was my mistake. Some of the people, as I mentioned, had come just for a lark and were intent on frightening their girlfriends or partners. Various stunts were going on in the dark and although I could see the funny side of it all, it wasn't really my

# HAUNTING

little group's scene. We had come to try out our individual psychic abilities. However, I did get the feeling of bones lying in rows along the length of the cellar. This was later confirmed by the leader. He said that the area had been where corpses had been kept until burial was arranged.

The final room was very beautiful. It was nowadays used as a conference area, with a large, highly polished table and grand chairs. The windows were high and majestic in appearance, with long heavy curtains. I sat at the head of this table with my back to the windows. There was very little space behind me, not enough for a human being. We started out trying our hand at automatic writing. This entails clearing your mind of any thought, difficult enough, and allowing spirit to control your hand which held the pencil poised over a piece of paper. We all shared our drawings and scribbles, with some finding that it produced some sort of contact or sensing. There was nothing of note for myself, although I enjoyed trying. It was the later period of medium links that was the best result for me. I became aware that a hair grip placed at the side of my head was being pulled down, just about to fall. Then a necklace that I was wearing had come undone and was falling slowly down my dress. The clasp was not faulty, in fact it was a rather hard one to do up and undo. I removed both the hair clip and the necklace. This occurrence was not new to me; it had happened once before when I had accompanied my friend Les in taking a group on a Shamanic day. Once these items were removed I felt fingers playing with my hair and heard children laughing. I reported this to the leader of this group and she asked if I were uncomfortable with their playing in this way. I said that it didn't worry me and we left it for a while. Later I said that it was enough and she encouraged the children to stop now, and they did. The evening became well worth going to after that. My family and friends all said that they would like to do this sort of thing again but with a specific group who really wanted to experience the psychic world. However nothing like this has come about to my knowledge.

# THE NARROW DOORWAY

The house next door to me is where Sharon lives. She was never very comfortable in the house, feeling that it was jinxed. It did have some sad history. The husband and wife had separated; the wife and their two sons remained in the house. The elder boy was on the borderline of genius. He was a strange boy of about eighteen or nineteen years of age. He dressed in a unique fashion and he acted strangely, with no eye contact. One day he just went to the park, taking some paraffin with which to douse his clothes and set fire to himself, resulting in his death. Not long after this his mother became ill with leukaemia and she died. The younger boy of seventeen was left. The house, of course, was sold.

I tried to reassure Sharon and suggested that she ask her priest to visit and bless the house. This she did, and felt a little better for a while. However, Sharon thought that the feeling had not disappeared altogether. We made arrangements for me to go in and try to clear it, when the rest of the family were out. As I did know the people who had lived there before and some of the unfortunately things that had gone on, I said that I would try. I had never done this kind of thing before, but I took a Bible and repeated a prayer and asked the spirit to return home as his family would be waiting for him. I knew that it was a male because I had vaguely seen him in the house previously. I moved about the house along with Sharon. She was also saying the prayer and asking him to go home, joining in with me. After a few months I asked her how the house felt lately. She replied that it seemed better on the whole, and what's more she hasn't complained or commented about anything for quite a while. This is something which I'm not eager to do generally; I tried because Sharon is a good friend.

I would like to say a few words about moving objects in your home or place of work, or wherever it's experienced. I think we have all had the feeling 'I'm sure I put that there, but it's turned up here.' You may think that you have not remembered correctly, and it may be so. However, sometimes it is spirit wanting you to be aware of them and that they are still with you.

# HAUNTING

In my front room there are quite a few figurines. One was of a woman in country clothes of the eighteen hundreds, a lovely figure in pink with a basket of varied flowers hoisted on her hip. I bought this piece along with other bits in a box at an auction many years ago, and it has always stood on top of my television set in the corner of the room by the window. My young grandchildren would often play together, all six of them, in that room, running around and mock fighting with my settee cushions. One day they came in to us to say that the figurine had 'flown' from the television on to the carpet. We all laughed and said that it was more likely that one of them had knocked it off. It had not broken, probably because at that time I had a very thick Chinese carpet on the floor. So no harm was done and it was replaced in its position. They insisted that they had not touched it, but we didn't really believe them. For many years after that they always repeated the same story, still saying that it wasn't them that knocked it off. I had never seen or sensed anything at all with the piece. I really liked it and although it had no markings underneath it that I could look up, I thought that one day I might have it valued.

Not long ago I was doing a spring clean and as I walked into the room it felt very stuffy, so I opened all the windows to let the air in. Now, I don't usually open the window by the television with the figurine on top, but this morning I did. The wind was blowing into the room and billowing the net curtains inwards; after a while my husband and I decided to go out and I closed all the windows hurriedly without noticing anything in particular, and out we went. On our return I stood looking at the front of the house, as one does at nothing, just idling the time while my husband opened the door, when I saw bits of something lying by the large bush I have in the front. Upon investigating we found 'my lady in pink' all broken up and beyond repair. My husband picked up the head to look at it, but said it seemed to wriggle out of his hands and fell back into the exact same place that he picked it up from. Now, this is a mystery because the television stands at least a couple of feet away from the window. What's more, the wind was blowing in, not out, and the net curtain would have stopped it. It did look more and more as if the lady had taken this opportunity to 'fly off' and out. I told my now adult grandchildren that I owed them an apology for not believing them all through the years.

The one other thing I actually saw move with my own eyes was a bandage. A friend of long standing had died after many a struggle with her health. I hadn't seen her for a long time as she had moved away. My husband and I weren't going far from home at that time due to health, though I did speak to her on the `phone. She was a strong character and always had a laugh or twinkle in her eye. I had always admired her spirit.

I used to bandage my feet before I went out for a walk. I kept the bandage on a bookshelf on one side of my bed when I didn't need it, properly wound up with no part of it hanging over the edge. I walked into the bedroom on retiring one night and went to the far side of the bed. As I looked across this large king-size bed, the bandage just lifted off the shelf before my eyes and fell to the floor. I hesitated for a moment and then went to retrieve the item and replace it, when I heard laughter. I recognised the laugh as belonging to my friend who had just died. It was just like her to play silly tricks. I laughed with her and said to her fading voice as she just went on her way, "We will leave it just here, please."

In my hallway I have a clay head which I had made many years ago. Very often my husband's hat sits at a cocky angle on its head. It has stayed on this head without moving, except when he is wearing it, for at least a year. About the same time as the figurine incident, the hat turned up on the floor by the stairs. Plant pots moved from one side of the window sill to the other side. All sorts of little incidents of that nature occurred. I was sure that someone was passing through, though I didn't know who.

In my church we get speakers and mediums giving talks and

words to ponder on. In many of the messages it is given that to be happy and contented you only have to look about the world and appreciate its wonders, the grass and flowers, trees, birds and so forth. I do look about me and hope that we, as a species, do not ruin this wonderful planet of ours. We do need to welcome each and every day no matter what the weather or what the day brings to us in our lives. This poem comes from opening my back door and breathing the fresh air and contemplating the scene; I try each day, definitely noting the seasons.

## Good Morning Lord

*Good morning, Lord, what a lovely day,*
*though the sky, tired of its heavy load,*
*releases gentle moisture*
*to cover the dark land and dusty road.*
*The earth grows green, refreshed with perfumed air,*
*sweetened by tulips blooming quickly there.*

*Good morning, Lord, what a lovely day,*
*though the breezy wind has many a sharp sting,*
*it sets the senses all aglow*
*with all the energy that it may bring,*
*breathing with renewed vigour and renewed life,*
*free from struggle and from strife.*

*Good morning, Lord, what a lovely day,*
*sun shines weakly from behind a cloudy sky.*
*Warmth slowly seeps through my closed lids*
*and patches of shadows slip silently by.*
*All the world lifts its sleepy head towards the light,*
*a golden crown that you have placed within our sight.*

## THE NARROW DOORWAY

*Good morning, Lord, what a lovely day,*
*the bright snow dazzles my peeping eyes,*
*all sparkling white, both soft and crisp,*
*drab dull earth now in mute disguise.*
*Oh let me learn to love each new and different day,*
*appreciate all you give as I go on my way.*

# Recently

I have in my house at the moment a young soldier who was in the First World War. I see him most days. When he first came, he seemed a bit angry at the fact that his life had been cut short by the war. He was a handsome young man with a dark moustache and a cap on his head. The cap looked a bit like an officer's but I felt that he was a private. I only see his head and shoulders but have the impression that he was about five feet eight inches in height and of average build, and that he was between twenty-three and twenty-six years of age. He told me that his name was George Turnbull. He was under the impression that his family were very upset because they didn't know what had happened to him. He had been reported missing, presumed dead. I replied that this had happened a long time ago and his family must have now passed into life on that side, so they would now know. It seemed that the thought had not occurred to him, so I do not know why they haven't got together with him. He continues to stay with me and give bits of information every now and then.

It appears that he was a London man, but I'm not sure if he was an only child or whether he had a younger sister. He was in the Royal Fusiliers. I have tried to confirm all of this information on the Internet records of the Great War and found that there were quite a few George Turnbulls; however I would need to pay to sign up for more. This at the moment is not possible, and I am not a great believer in putting money over the `net. I'm a bit old-fashioned, I guess. However, George seems less angry nowadays. I do talk to him and tell him that I tried to identify him, but at the moment that's as far as I can go.

A young man, who comes to me for a reading now and then, came recently with questions in his mind. I cannot give any real answers - none have been given to me - but I can give some reassurance and guidelines. At the time, I also saw a guide who was with him. It was an old-fashioned footballer, again with the typical moustache that was popular around the early twentieth century. He had a striped cap on his head which to me looked like a cricketer's cap. I couldn't reconcile the two until I asked my husband about the hats that were once worn by sportsmen of that era. He said that footballers of that time all wore caps that looked like the ones that cricketers used. So I could accept that he was a footballer and was guiding this young man.

I haven't yet mentioned all the little everyday things that probably happen in your lives as well as mine. They are so fleeting that you either take no notice or think to yourself, 'Well, that's life' or 'It's coincidence'. These can be little things, like the time I was driving to work one morning. I have an opportunity to go various ways to get there and make the choice as I go, according to traffic. One morning, as I was waiting at the lights a 'voice' said in my head, "Turn left here." Usually the clearer route is straight on and then turn left. I ignored this voice, thinking I was just being silly because everything had been clear. Oh dear, I went straight on and did my usual route and found an accident had happened and I was stuck right behind an ambulance and police cars. Mental note to myself: listen to my voices, they know more.

Once a fortnight I have a gardener who comes to help with the upkeep of the garden. As he was leaving the other day, his hands full of gardening equipment, the gate at the side of the house opened up for him. It is a latch type of gate. He called to me and asked if I had a ghost. I told him yes, and most places or people do. We laughed and remarked that at least it was a helpful ghost.

# Questions and Musings with God

*Muse: If a black hole came and swallowed the Earth,*
*you would have every soul in Heaven.*
*Would there be enough room?*

*God: There is enough room for every living thing.*

*Muse: Everything? Even beetles, bugs and spiders?*
*I don't like spiders,*
*would they keep away from me there?*

*God: Yes, if you don't want them near.*

*Muse: God, I don't really want the world to be swallowed up.*

*God: I know.*

*Muse: I have a pain, you could stop it,*
*why does there have to be pain?*

*God: It's part of the Earth, part of Earthly being.*

*Muse: You sent your son to Earth, he suffered,*
*isn't that enough?*
*Those thorns, beatings and just hanging there.*

*God: Yes, he had to suffer.*

*Muse: But He was your son, someone special,*
*he knew what everything was about,*
*we don't.*
*We're not your sons and daughters – Oh, hmm…*

*God: You are all my children.*

*Muse: Yes, I suppose we are.*
*He was your son and was in pain,*
*so it goes for us too. Okay.*
*But it's your world, you made everything,*
*so why can't we go back to the Garden of Eden?*
*The sins of the mother, repaid by mankind,*
*it was a pretty hefty price to pay,*
*for one mistake.*

*God: That's another story.*

*Muse: Couldn't you forgive Eve and give her another chance?*
*Take us back to the garden!*

*God: That, my child, is exactly where you are going.*

The conclusion that I draw from this is that some day, some time, we shall return to that garden. Maybe God will give us another chance. Or, as the Mayans who once lived in South America say, we already have had four or five worlds and they are waiting for this one to collapse and then God will start everything up again. Whatever happens, it will be an interesting life and afterlife, for all of us.

GOD BLESS EVERYONE

# The Seven Principles of Spiritualism

These were given to us by spirit as guidelines. I write them for any reader who is not familiar with this belief. The word God is to recognise a conscience or force for positive, for truth and above all for love.

1  The Fatherhood of God.
2  The brotherhood of man.
3  The communion of spirits and the ministry of angels.
4  The continuous existence of the human soul.
5  Personal responsibility.
6  Compensation and retribution hereafter, for all good and evil done on Earth.
7  Eternal progress open to every human soul.

# If you have enjoyed this book...

Local Legend is committed to publishing the very best spiritual writing. You might also enjoy:


**SIMPLY SPIRITUAL**

Jacqui Rogers (ISBN 978-1-907203-75-6)

The 'spookies' started contacting Jacqui when she was a child and never gave up until, at last, she developed her psychic talents and became the successful international medium she is now. This is a powerful and moving account of her difficult life and her triumph over adversity, with many great stories of her spiritual readings.

The book was a Finalist in The People's Book Prize national awards.


**AURA CHILD**

A I Kaymen (ISBN 978-1-907203-71-8)

One of the most astonishing books ever written, telling the true story of a genuine Indigo child. Genevieve grew up in a normal London family but from an early age realised that she had very special spiritual and psychic gifts. She saw the energy fields around living things, read people's thoughts and even found herself slipping through time, able to converse with the spirits of those who had lived in her neighbourhood. This is an uplifting and inspiring book for what it tells us about the nature of our minds.

# A SINGLE PETAL

## Oliver Eade (ISBN 978-1-907203-42-8)

Winner of the national Local Legend Spiritual Writing Competition, this page-turner is a novel of murder, politics and passion set in ancient China. Yet its themes of loyalty, commitment and deep personal love are every bit as relevant for us today as they were in past times. The author is an expert on Chinese culture and history, and his debut adult novel deserves to become a classic.

# THE QUIRKY MEDIUM

## Alison Wynne-Ryder (ISBN 978-1-907203-47-3)

Alison is the co-host of the TV show *Rescue Mediums*, in which she puts herself in real danger to free homes of lost and often malicious spirits. Yet she is a most reluctant medium, afraid of ghosts! This is her amazing and often very funny autobiography, taking us 'back stage' of the television production as well as describing how she came to discover the psychic gifts that have brought her an international following.

Winner of the Silver Medal in the national Wishing Shelf Book Awards.

# 5P1R1T R3V3L4T10N5

## Nigel Peace (ISBN 978-1-907203-14-5)

With descriptions of more than a hundred proven prophetic dreams and many more everyday synchronicities, the author shows us that, without doubt, we can know the future and that everyone can receive genuine spiritual guidance for our lives' challenges. World-renowned biologist Dr Rupert Sheldrake has endorsed this book as "...vivid and fascinating... pioneering research..." and it was national runner-up in The People's Book Prize awards.

# CELESTIAL AMBULANCE

## Ann Matkins (ISBN 978-1-907203-45-9)

A brave and delightful comedy novel. Having died of cancer, Ben wakes up in the afterlife looking forward to a good rest, only to find that everyone is expected to get a job! He becomes the driver of an ambulance (with a mind of her own), rescuing the spirits of others who have died suddenly and delivering them safely home. This book is as thought-provoking as it is entertaining.

# RAINBOW CHILD

## S L Coyne (ISBN 978-1-907203-92-3)

Beautifully written in language that is alternately lyrical and childlike, this is the story of young Rebekah and the people she discovers as her family settles in a new town far from their familiar home. As dark family secrets begin to unravel, her life takes many turns both delightful and terrifying as the story builds to a tragic and breathless climax that just keeps on going. This book shows us how we look at others who are 'different'. Through the eyes of Rebekah, writing equally with passion and humour, we see the truth of human nature...

# TAP ONCE FOR YES

## Jacquie Parton (ISBN 978-1-907203-62-6)

This extraordinary book offers powerful evidence of human survival after death. When Jacquie's son Andrew suddenly committed suicide, she was devastated. But she was determined to find out whether his spirit lived on, and began to receive incredible yet undeniable messages from him... Several others also then described deliberate attempts at spirit contact. This is a story of astonishing love and courage, as Jacquie fought her own grief and others' doubts in order to prove to the world that her son still lives.

# SPINACH SOUP FOR THE WALLS

## Lynne Harkes (ISBN 978-1-907203-46-6)

Gold Medal winner in the national Wishing Shelf Book Awards, this is a message of hope for anyone in despair. When we see our troubles as opportunities for growth, we can turn our lives around and "recognise the remarkable in the ordinary". Lynne has lived in many wonderful and colourful places, from South America to the jungle of Gabon in West Africa, and she describes graphically the resilience of the native peoples and the magnificence of the natural world. Yet she found herself retreating into unhappiness and isolation. This beautifully written book is the story of how she fought to rediscover her own spirituality and find a new way of thinking.

These titles are all available as paperbacks and eBooks.
Further details and extracts of these and many
other beautiful books may be seen at

*www.local-legend.co.uk*

Lightning Source UK Ltd.
Milton Keynes UK
UKOW06f2141191015

260963UK00001B/1/P

# THE NARROW
# DOORWAY